Looking for Home: A Lesbian Life in America

Dr. Gail S. Bernstein

Published by Ralph Bernstein, 2024.

Table of Contents

Dedicated to all who are different and looking for home

Introduction

I had long admired my sister Gail for her passion, her dedication and her courage. I'd known since we were young adults that she was a lesbian, and I was often impressed by her unwavering fight for LGBT rights, both for herself and others, despite the frequent frustrations she inevitably encountered. She had long been an outspoken advocate for the LGBT community, primarily in Colorado where she lived for many years, often writing essays and columns for local LGBT publications.

Gail held a doctorate in psychology, and her career spanned a variety of roles, including teacher, group home parent, technical writer, and developmental disabilities specialist. She authored a book, <u>Human Services? That must be so rewarding: A Practical Guide for Professional Development,</u> and was one of four co-authors of another book, <u>Proactive Vocational Habilitation.</u>

But I believe one of her most significant professional roles was as a psychologist in private practice in Denver, serving many LGBT clients. And she achieved all this despite having to spend most of her adult life battling multiple sclerosis.

After Gail passed away, my brother and I handled going through her possessions, saving some items, donating and disposing of others. I ended up with Gail's laptop.

On it I found much of her writing, including numerous essays and columns, as well as notes to herself about writing. And to my surprise, I also discovered several parts of an unfinished memoir.

While I always knew Gail to be brilliant, I was particularly impressed by her writing. Through it, she communicated with a distinct voice noteworthy for her passion, her clarity of thought and, especially, her humanity. And she was unafraid to reveal herself, writing openly and honestly about everything from her personal relationships to her medical struggles.

My immediate reaction was that this voice should be preserved and heard by as wide an audience as possible. And I could think of no better monument to my sister, and no better legacy for her, than to compile her writing into a book.

I am retired from a career in journalism, and I decided to use the editing skills I had developed to accomplish this task. It truly was a labor of love.

Gail wrote not just about LGBT issues, but other topics as well, ranging from abortion to healthcare and aging. Her thoughts on these issues were just as wise and insightful. And her personal recollections bring into sharp focus what it means to be a non-heterosexual person in America today.

Several of her essays sprang out of the fight over Amendment Two in Colorado, an anti-LGBT initiative approved by the state's voters in 1992 but declared unconstitutional several years later. While Amendment Two is history, Gail's comments on the issues involved are timeless and are included in this book.

I have tried to organize it all into a logical order, and what I hope is a coherent whole, interspersing parts of her personal story with her essays on issues. I've also added an afterward at the end.

I did very little editing of Gail's actual writing, for two reasons. First, Gail was a good writer whose work didn't need much editing. But more importantly, I wanted her voice to come through.

I hope that you enjoy this book. And I hope her words will cause readers to think, to consider their own positions and values, and perhaps spur them to action in the battle for equal rights for all, regardless of background or sexual orientation. Nothing would have pleased Gail more.

Ralph Bernstein

Chapter One: Fitting In

If i have one story to tell it's about feeling like an outsider, like I don't fit in, and finding a better environment, a place where I do fit in

I have always wanted to be connected, to be heard, to be accepted, to fit in, but like most of us also wanted to be unique, to stand out.

I have always wanted to fit in because I often felt like I didn't.

It is only in retrospect that I have been able to articulate what I wanted so clearly: I could not have done so in my youth.

I have always wanted to change the world by being helpful.

My generation believed we could change the world, make it better. I was 13 when John Kennedy famously said, "Ask not what your country can do for you, ask what you can do for your country." My high school senior class motto was "I am the master of my fate: I am the captain of my soul."

I grew up believing that you could make a difference by teaching. My father had earned his undergraduate and master's degrees before he enlisted in the Army in 1942. He was a high school teacher until I was 13 and taught in a low-income neighborhood in Detroit. He held a doctorate in education; his dissertation research was based on figuring out why kids made the arithmetic mistakes that they made. He then moved on to become a math curriculum consultant for Wayne County, which included Detroit and 43 other school districts. My mother had completed two years of college during World War II and taught religious school when I was small. After my youngest brother was born, she went back to school part-time and finished her undergraduate degree in speech education at the end of my sophomore year in high school, then started teaching full-time the following year.

I spent much of my childhood buried in a book. There were always books in the house, and both my parents were readers. They never placed any limits on what I read. Browsing through their books is how I found Anne Frank's diary and how I developed a love of mysteries, starting with

Agatha Christie's classics, a love that continues to this day (though now I lean more towards mysteries with more fully-realized detectives and other characters, and mostly I read mysteries by women.) Somewhere in late adolescence I found science fiction and dreamed of going to the moon. Books introduced me to other worlds and let me escape the less desirable parts of the world I was in. I was the oldest of three and much loved, but my mother sometimes yelled at me and I hated being yelled at. I can't remember specific incidents now, just that to this day I still have trouble when people yell at me.

The house we lived in from the time I was five until I left for college was in one of the numerous developments that was built to accommodate growing families in the early 1950s. It had a small dining room, living room, kitchen and bathroom on the first floor as well as my parents' bedroom and another room they set up as a family room. The upstairs was an attic that my father and grandfather finished into two bedrooms. The smaller was mine and you had to walk through it to get to the larger bedroom which housed my two brothers, only one of whom had been born when we first moved in. It was the first full house my parents had ever lived in. They both grew up in New York City apartments and lived in apartments in Detroit and then a duplex before buying the house. It didn't seem like a small house when I was growing up: It was just home. There were times, however, when it did seem crowded. One of my most successful efforts as a comedian occurred one morning when all five of us were trying to get into the bathroom to get ready for work and school. My middle brother was, as usual, in the bathroom primping. I tore up four small pieces of paper, wrote the numbers one through four on them and gave one each to my parents and my other brother.

My first experience of not fitting in, being the outsider, was in grade school. I was smart, Jewish, and clumsy. One year I ran the slowest 50-yard dash in the class. By eighth grade I was also the tallest and fat - not obese, but at 153 pounds definitely big compared to my classmates.

In addition, though I wasn't conscious in grade school of receiving special treatment, my teachers certainly knew that my father also taught in the Detroit schools. By eighth grade my classmates were doing all the latest dances at our sock hops. I would have loved to be on the dance floor but hadn't a clue how to dance or how to learn. The one girl friend I had through the latter part of grade school was someone else who didn't fit in because her mother was divorced, and single moms were a rarity in our district. She also, though I didn't realize it at the time, had a last name that almost certainly spoke of the Mideast, so that also made her different.

There was one place during those years that I fit in, and that was at Temple. We were members of Temple Beth El, the Reform Jewish congregation where my mother taught religious school. My brothers and I all went to the religious school on weekends. I sang in the choir when I was in the 7th and 8th grades and became the third girl in the history of the congregation to have a bat mitzvah. It was a place where it was just fine to be smart and Jewish, and I loved going there.

When I finished high school and went to college, I attended the University of Wisconsin. I went on to graduate school because I realized I could not have the impact on people's lives, the ability to improve them that I wanted to have, without those letters after my name. But I hadn't thought it through completely. I wanted to be a clinical psychologist. The University of Wisconsin-Madison's doctoral program in clinical psychology was designed to train researchers, which is not what I wanted. At the time I applied to graduate school, I thought I wanted to be a full-time clinician. And I didn't want to move. So I looked on the program I went through as an alternative way to become a psychologist—my major professor was a licensed clinical psychologist. I got both more and less than I'd bargained for.

The assumption that permeated graduate school—and I do not believe it was specific to my department, I believe it was university-wide—was that we were expected to be the best and the brightest, expected to make significant contributions to our field, expected to develop national reputations just as many of our professors had done. Or at least some of us were. I realized later that the ones who did not show that promise were the ones who were, at least the women, more likely to be sexually harassed, less likely to get faculty attention and guidance.

The contributions could take many forms in developmental disabilities: significant contributions to special education, to advocacy, to behavior change. And, as difficult and flawed as some of the faculty were, after I finished and started having contact with people who'd been trained in other places, I came to realize that I had, in fact, gotten an excellent education in addition to earning those letters after my name.

My first eight years out of graduate school I headed to some extent in the direction I'd been pointed in by my training. I wrote a lot and published, though much of it was not research. I'd learned that research was not my passion. Writing, translating new knowledge, making it accessible to practitioners, was my forte. I loved staff training, teaching people how to observe and change using positive behavioral change methods. But I also became disenchanted with the constantly increasing pressure to generate more income. I didn't have the marketing skills or the networking skills to do that well; I hadn't been trained for it.

So I decided to leave university-based institutes, shift gears, and go into clinical practice—but not with people with developmental disabilities. I'm not sure I was going toward something so much as going away from what had become an increasingly uncomfortable work environment. With exquisitely bad timing, I entered private practice psychotherapy just as managed care was making major inroads into how private clinicians were being reimbursed. And, once again, my lack of marketing skills worked against me.

Chapter Two: Realization

It wasn't until I was 24 that I figured out the other way I was different. Then I went to work in a group home program for adolescents and some children with emotional difficulties. At first, I rotated filling in for night staff at the two homes the agency ran at that time. My introduction to the other staff was at a touch football game, where one of the women, another new staff member, caught my eye. She was a daytime staff member at one of the homes where I worked night shift, and I always stayed for breakfast when she came in to relieve me. She made the best breakfasts in the world. We soon started spending lots of our off time together, talking late into the night. I learned that she had been a nun for eight years and was just a year out of the convent when we met. She moved in with me on New Year's Eve, and I made my sexual interest in her clear fairly soon. It took her another three months to reciprocate. She'd been well taught in the convent to avoid "particular friendships." During the first three months we lived together, sometimes we slept in separate beds and sometimes in the same bed, but always in pajamas and barely touching. Then one night she kissed me, and the world changed forever. Love songs finally made sense: I was 24 and head over heels in a way I'd never dreamed was possible.

In retrospect my attraction to women had been there for a long time. My best friend in high school and I spent a lot of time convincing ourselves we were mad for two boys we'd picked out, but I suspect there was considerable attraction there. And for my part, it became clear in retrospect that I'd been trying to convince myself that I loved the boy and that, given my subsequent experiences with women, I had not had the intense feelings for him that I once thought might be there.

I was clearly in love with my best friend in college, though it was a couple of decades later before we both acknowledged what had happened and had a conversation about it. She was clearly heterosexual, and I was lesbian but yet to realize it

Then I went on a camping trip with a former high school student the summer after she graduated and I left teaching. I was 24 and she was 18, and she seduced me. I was an incredibly naive 24-year-old in spite of having experimented with men sexually for a year or so before that trip. We were in the tent one night and she pretended to be asleep as she explored my body. The relationship ended badly later that year, but it left me with the knowledge that I was drawn to women in a way that I never felt about men. Contrary to the persistent stereotype, I don't hate men, never did. I had some pleasant sexual experiences with men, but never had an orgasm. That may have been due to my lack of knowledge about my body and the male lack of knowledge about how to treat a woman, but it never felt completely right to me until I made love with a woman.

During the group home days politics was the backdrop. We didn't talk about it, but it was always there. Most if not all the men working in the programs were conscientious objectors, but they didn't talk about it. Mostly we gathered in our time off to get stoned and watch movies or just talk.

I was opposed to the war in Vietnam but never actively protested it, for two reasons. One is that some people just mouthed the words they heard from some of the leaders of the protest movements like "university complicity" in the war. I believe some protestors believed the university was in support of the war machine, but I also thought some were simply following the herd. The more important reason I didn't join the protests is that I had friends on both sides of the issues. One friend and his fiancé were prepared to leave for Canada if his conscientious objector status was not approved. My closest friend during my undergraduate years married a man whom I knew and liked while he was on a seven-day rest and recreation league from his infantry work in Vietnam. He came home, finished his undergraduate work while in ROTC, and retired from the military after a long career in the Army.

Unlike many of the antiwar protestors, I never saw soldiers as the enemy. I always thought the war decisions were made in Washington and then carried out by men who either were drafted or enlisted because they felt it was their patriotic duty to serve.

Back to my ex-nun. We were both still involved with men while we were beginning our relationship and were identifying as bisexual, but the men gradually dropped out of the picture. The first time I came out to a heterosexual friend who knew us and the men in our lives, she said, "Oh, now it all makes sense." I'd been grousing passionately to her about how badly a man was treating my partner, so much so that it had seemed all out of proportion until I told her that my partner and I were not just good friends.

She and I were isolated the first few years we were together. We knew one other lesbian couple, but they drank a lot, and we knew we didn't want to be like them. We didn't have any experience with other women like us and didn't know how to find them. Then I started graduate school full time. My first statistics instructor was a lesbian who introduced us to the lesbian switchboard, which had a small office at the University YMCA. It consisted of a lending library, a few slightly seedy chairs and a couch, and an office with a desk and chair and a phone. We became volunteers at the Switchboard and worked regular shifts at the office where we answered calls from women looking for help or community. Suddenly, we were part of a community and not an isolated couple. The Switchboard also sponsored social events; I remember one year we made dozens of cookies that were two overlapping women's symbols for the Valentine's Day dance.

There was a very active women's music circuit in the 70s that gave a forum to lesbian performers. When one of the women's music stars came to town, we all gathered for their concerts, usually at a place called Freedom House. It was a large open room with a slightly raised platform at one end that served as the stage. We took blankets, drinks, and munchies and staked out a piece of the floor. We were in our 20s and limber, so the floor was not a problem. My god, that was a long time ago. No way I could sit on the floor for a concert these days.

Another important gathering place was a gay bar called The Back Door. The entrance was indeed a back door off an alley. The first thing you saw on entering was a mural of Dorothy and Toto from the Wizard of Oz, with Dorothy telling Toto, "I don't think we're in Kansas anymore." Thursday was women's night at The Back Door, so a group of us would gather there for a few hours every Thursday. It was a space where butch-femme couples hung out as well as our 20-something group of t-shirted and blue-jeaned women. The different types of lesbians rarely interacted; we all were there for a safe space where we could be who we were. The only bad times came when an out-of-town businessman would wander in by mistake and try to pick up one of us. What the men never realized is that a large group of overly protective lesbians were in the next booth listening to them and preparing to pounce if our friend appeared to be in need of protection. Fortunately, it didn't happen while I was there, but it was an ever-present danger.

The Switchboard also had a Speaker's Bureau. Periodically we'd get a call from a college instructor or another organization that wanted speakers about being lesbian or gay. We'd tromp off to the event together with some men from the Gay Men's Crisis Line to sit in front of the class or group and tell our stories. This was mostly about putting a face on those queer words and making us less scary and more human. I signed up to speak to groups that were an hour or more from Madison. Even in a community as liberal as Madison, graduate students are still vulnerable, and I didn't want to advertise too close to home.

In addition, my major professor's daughter was a lesbian: I didn't know her personally, but the lesbian community was a small town, and I knew about her. What I didn't know was whether her father knew about her, and I didn't want to find out.

A year or two after we moved to Denver, we were in a group of six women attending a very early Pride Parade in Cheeseman Park. Our picnic of various munchies and a bottle of nice wine was interrupted by one of the Park Police, who lectured us at length about the wine and how it was illegal at city parks. One of my friends had the presence of mind to talk the officer down and take the wine to her car. We were left alone after that encounter, but it was a reminder that gays and lesbians were always in danger of police harassment. Sure, the wine was illegal, but if half of our group had been male, the lecture might not have happened, or might have taken the form of a simple reminder to put away the wine.

In Denver, we lived through the years of the AIDS epidemic. The epidemic came closest to home in 1991 when a dear friend found himself in the hospital. Fortunately, he recovered enough to make a will and create powers of attorney so that his partner of over 20 years would be treated legally as the life partner he was in reality. Chuck lived well over a year after his initial illness, but this was at a time when the drugs that would make the disease a chronic illness instead of an immediately fatal one were not yet available.

Then the fight for gay and lesbian rights came to Colorado. By that time, I was already an out part of the lesbian and gay community. I used picture ads for my psychotherapy practice in gay publications. (This was before online advertising made most print ads obsolete.) I was writing regularly for the local lesbian paper and occasionally for the gay press. I treated a lot of internalized homophobia and wrote about treating gay and lesbian issues in behavior therapy publications. I had not, however, actively worked for gay rights until 1991.

That year, the voters in Denver defeated a challenge to an ordinance that prohibited discrimination, including discrimination based on sexual orientation. The following year, a group called Colorado for Family Values was able to get an initiative on the state ballot that, if enacted, would have prohibited the state and its municipalities from adopting or enforcing these types of anti-discrimination laws.

The campaign for the measure was vitriolic, to say the least.

It passed the same night Clinton was elected to his first term as President, but it was immediately challenged in court and was not implemented pending judicial challenges. Nearly four years later

Amendment Two was declared unconstitutional. During the years leading up to Amendment Two and for several years thereafter, I had a psychotherapy practice that served primarily, though not exclusively, lesbian and gay individuals.

On election night, my partner and I were among the hundreds of people at No on Amendment Two headquarters waiting for the vote to come in. We started out elated that Clinton, who had made pro-gay statements, was elected handily. Then the votes on Amendment Two came in, and it became clear that this bigoted measure was going to pass, in spite of what voters had told pollsters about how they were going to vote. Too many people found it easy to lie to the pollsters and vote "yes" for the Amendment.

The following spring I went to a concert given by a lesbian and gay chorus called Harmony. We were in the balcony and could see much of the audience on the ground floor. At one point, the chorus sang "Do You Hear the People Sing" from the musical Les Miserables. However, they changed the words. Instead of "...it is the song of a people who will not be slaves again" they sang, "...this is the music of a people who will not be shamed again." When we heard those words, the crowd came to its feet as if on cue and the applause at the end was ferocious. We'd had enough and were ready to take on all comers.

The week of the election brought me some of the hardest work I have ever done. After the vote was in, I had a steady stream of people in my office asking "Why?" Why did my parents vote against me?" "Why did people scream obscenities at me while I stood on a street corner with a "Yes on Amendment Two sign?" "Why did the preacher give a sermon condemning me to hell?" I didn't realize how traumatized I was until several weeks later at a professional conference. Some of my friends from around the country asked me what it was like in Denver during the election. As I started to tell them, I realized that I sounded very much like the traumatized clients I'd been seeing in my therapy office.

It's been more than twenty years since that time, but impact still there. I still feel like I have to apologize for living in Colorado Springs, because that's where the groups that started and promulgated the amendment were located. That's where the bigotry lived.

Chapter Three: Abortion Is Not Always Agonizing

Sometimes discussions of abortion include acknowledgement that it is women who have them, sometimes they do not. When it is acknowledged that a woman may choose to have an abortion, her choice is often described as one that is "anguished" or "agonizing" or "heartbreaking."

The subtext here is that women are not allowed to choose abortions unless they anguish over the choice. They are not allowed to make abortion a decision based on questions such as whether they can afford to support a child, whether they would be good parents or even whether they want to be parents at all, God forbid women should make rational decisions that include consideration of what an abortion would mean for them. This is nonsense, but unfortunately powerful nonsense too often accepted instead of challenged. To deny that a woman might choose abortion for practical reasons is to deny that women have the right to consider the impact of a pregnancy on themselves.

A pregnancy always involves the woman who is pregnant and the life she carries within her. The choice of whether to terminate the pregnancy should always include consideration of the choice on both the woman and the life she carries. To ignore the potential impact on a woman of carrying a pregnancy to term is to say that a woman is no more than a vessel for carrying pregnancies.

Another national conversation about abortion has been about what happens to fetal tissue. As usual, the women who are pregnant and make choices about what to do are largely ignored. That is no surprise, as those who are opposed to abortion prefer to see women simply as vessels rather than as individuals with thoughts and feelings about what is happening to their bodies. As long as those of us who have made choices about abortion stay silent, the antichoice voices will set the terms of the conversation.

The only way to convey the variety in how women cope emotionally and practically with whether to choose abortion is for many of us to tell our stories publicly. Here is mine.

I was in my 20s when my IUD failed, and I became pregnant. It was the brief time in my life when I was sexually active with a woman and a man, before I had acknowledged to myself that my primary emotional and physical bonds were with women, and I was confused about who I was and what I wanted. I had begun to realize that I didn't want to be a parent, and I was certain I didn't want to be one then. I was making very little money and would have resented the loss of independence and financial struggle that would have accompanied becoming a parent at that time. I didn't make the decision lightly, but it was serious rather than agonizing. The man I was involved with paid for half of the abortion and was willing to go with me, but I declined. Instead, the woman I was involved with, who would become my first long-term lesbian partner, accompanied me.

Making the appointment was simple. The staff made sure that I wanted to have the abortion and explained the procedure to me, including possible risks and recovery instructions.

The comic relief in this otherwise serious situation was provided by the woman who was there to support me. Because she worked in the same group home I did, a program for adolescents with emotional problems, and had been present at a fifteen-year-old's abortion, the clinic staff knew her and let her be present at mine. But seeing me in pain during the procedure was more than she could bear; she fainted, landed on the floor, and ended up in the bed next to mine in the recovery room. Fortunately, we both made a complete recovery.

I was also fortunate to have become pregnant at a time when abortion had become legal. Birth control was available legally. There were no required explanations by the doctors about the so-called negative consequences of abortion, there was no required waiting period, there were no anti-abortion picketers shouting at the clinic entrance and an ultrasound was not required. The year was 1972, just a few short months before Roe v. Wade made abortion legal in all 50 states, and it was already legal in Wisconsin, where I lived at the time.

This is a different time. Today, that adolescent girl and I would have found the path to a legal abortion much more difficult. One of her parents would have had to give the legally required consent. Both of us would have been required to have an ultrasound, to listen to a health professional give us information that is designed to discourage abortion and to wait 24 hours after we received the information before having the procedure. Many more forms of birth control are available than in 1972, but they are still less available to women with low incomes than to women with high ones.

According to the Guttmacher Institute, 17 states require some type of counseling, 26 require waiting periods, 25 require one or both parents of a minor to consent to an abortion and an additional 13 require that one or both parents be notified. Many states have additional limits, such as what private insurance may cover and whether so-called "partial birth" abortions are allowed.

Abortion should not have to be an agonizing choice to be socially acceptable. There is something seriously wrong with a country that is so blatantly willing to take control of a woman's body and so blindly assumes that all adolescents have parents who are available to make decisions for their daughters. let alone make decisions that take their daughters' health and desires into account.

And if the politicians who would defund Planned Parenthood were serious about reducing the incidence of abortion, they would give more funding to the one organization we know provides family planning services to women who cannot afford to find them elsewhere.

Roxanne Gay reminds us that women have historically gone underground for pregnancy termination and will do so again if no legal means are available. It is to our shame that women may be forced to go underground in this country once again.

Chapter Four: I'll Be Nice to Them

Real change, change that endures, doesn't happen in large and dramatic ways. It happens in small pieces, a little at a time, a day at a time. The real heroes, the real-world changes, are not the people described in history books. They are people with stories like this one.

It was the end of the summer, almost time for school to start. Her daughter, who had always been a friendly, popular child, had been shunned by most of the other seventh graders the previous year. When the mother mentioned school would be starting soon, her daughter burst into tears. A little probing uncovered the reason: a few weeks earlier the child had discovered why she'd been an outcast the previous year. It seems a female classmate had started a rumor that the girl was a lesbian.

Bless this child's mother, who's first reaction was to say, "You're mine and I love you." Then they had the conversation about sexual orientation. Her daughter said, "I'm not a lesbian, but if I ever meet anyone who is, I'll be nice to them."

This child learned a couple of important lessons. First, and most important, she learned her mother's love was not conditional. She learned her mother cares for her no matter who she loves. She also learned a painful lesson about how it feels to be an outcast. Fortunately, she came away from it wanting to avoid making anyone else an outcast, wanting to avoid making anyone else feel bad.

What if this child was in fact a lesbian? What if she had just started to realize she was having the same feelings about girls that most of her female classmates were having about boys? She would have learned from her classmates that it wasn't okay to be who she was. She would have learned that, if she wanted to be accepted, she'd have to hide an important part of herself.

What if her mother's reaction had been, "Of course you're not, you're just going through a phase."? She would have learned her mother would not love her unless she was heterosexual.

We live in a world where some children learn it is a bad thing to feel love and attraction for someone of the same gender, a world where some parents say it is acceptable to punish people for who they are, for who they love. It is a world where too many people believe the gender of those you love is more important than the quality of your relationships. The appalling result is that our lesbian and gay youth attempt suicide two to three times more often than their heterosexual peers, that as many as 30 percent of the completed teen suicides in this country are committed by gay and lesbian adolescents.

Fortunately, we also live in a world where there are mothers who respond to the possibility their children are different by saying, "You're mine and I love you." And we live in a world where a child who has been treated as an outcast has decided she will not treat people badly because they are different from her, that she will be nice to those who are not like her. We need more mothers and daughters like these two, more fathers and sons like them as well. They are our best chance to create a world where children who are different no longer feel abandoned, where children who are different no longer rush to end lives full of pain. They are the real heroes, the real creators of enduring change. They are our best hope for the future.

Chapter Five: Why I Won't Go Back in the Closet

Here's what the homophobes want us to do now that Amendment 2 has passed. They want us to go back in the closet. They want us to pretend we do not exist. They want us to be scapegoats, to serve as targets, to grieve quietly when we are fired, to be silent when we are called names. They do not want to acknowledge their responsibility when we are beaten for being different. They want us to roll over and submit, to learn to devalue ourselves as intensely as they devalue us, to tacitly accept the grouping of people into positive and negative categories based on who we love, on who we find sexually attractive.

Sorry, folks. I won't do it. I won't go back in the closet. I won't pretend I have something to hide, something wrong with me, so that others will be more comfortable.

I won't let another generation of professionals come of age without role models. At a professional meeting two weeks after Amendment 2 passed, a young doctoral student wrote me a note to say: "I wanted to thank you for wearing the pink triangle. I saw it earlier and felt good/safe/home/welcome/whatever. I do not feel safe being out in my program, but I hope someday to be able to do what you do."

I won't let another generation of relationships come of age without role models. I won't devalue my relationship by hiding it or cloaking it in euphemisms. One night in December in the women's country bar, two young women on their way out stopped by our table to say how good my partner and I looked on the dance floor. When we were their age, there were no gray-haired, middle-aged lesbians we could look to in the same way. How can I truly celebrate and honor the depth and richness of 21 years if I cannot say it out loud?

I won't go back in the closet because the quiet ones need those of us who are out to stay out. Every community leader I spoke with after the election agreed that those most at risk, most in need, are the quiet ones. I do not pretend to be particularly courageous: My livelihood and my home are not at risk. I am self-employed and most of my clients are lesbian or gay, so I'm not going to be fired for my sexual orientation. We own our home, so I am not going to be evicted. If I don't stay out, who will?

I won't go back in the closet because it takes too much energy to hide, and life is too short to waste it that way.

When I was a child, I learned the Talmud asks "If I am not for myself, who will be for me? If I am for myself alone, what am I? And if not now, when?" That, finally, is why I will not go back in the closet. Life is finite: if not now, when?

Chapter Six: The Price of Prejudice

We learn prejudice early in life. We learn it when a parent makes a nasty remark about "greasers" or "chinks" or "niggers." We learn it from the tone of voice used when a child is called "faggot" or "dyke" or "queer." We learn it whenever we hear "girls can't do that," or "boys don't cry." Prejudice is emotional. It is, according to Webster, "an unwarranted bias." We learn many prejudices before we are old enough to be able to critically analyze what we are learning.

Prejudice begets more prejudice. People who are repeatedly attacked or judged unfairly often respond by hunkering down behind the barricades and making unwarranted judgments about their attackers. That's a natural reaction, and it perpetuates the problem.

Several commentators expressed surprise at the anger expressed by opponents of Amendment Two after the election. From a psychological perspective, the anger was predictable. People get angry when you do something hurtful to them, even if they know you are going to do it. They get really angry if you do something hurtful and it's a surprise. Amendment Two opponents were taken by surprise when it passed. The polls had been suggesting it would fail right up until the day before the election. In addition, the gay, lesbian and bisexual citizens of cities that already had civil rights based on sexual orientation lost that protection. When you take something away from a person, whether it's a job, a possession, or a legal protection, anger is a natural response.

The human cost of prejudice is enormous, both for individuals and for society. I see the costs of prejudice based on sexual orientation every day in my psychotherapy practice. I also see the costs paid by my friends and colleagues. I see parents who have lost custody of their children, deeply religious individuals who have been rejected by their home congregations, and far too many good people who tried to kill themselves to silence the pain of social condemnation and rejection. I also see too many people who have been physically assaulted because they were gay or lesbian, or someone thought they were, and many more who live in fear.

I'm very fortunate: my personal exposure to the more vitriolic expressions of prejudice has been limited. Nonetheless, I do have my share of fears. Some of them come from my observations of what's happened to clients and friends. Some of them come from experience. I have a collection of mail, nearly all of it anonymous, from people who have had something negative to say about my public opposition to Amendment Two, my sexual orientation, or both. I can't tell you too much about the worst letter I've received: most of it is too obscene to be printed here. It says, in part, "What you really need is a long hot f*** with a man." That's a scary letter.

For several months after Amendment Two passed, I was afraid to go anywhere near Colorado Springs. I had some personal business that required a drive through Colorado Springs a few months after the election, and I took our dog with me for protection. Irrational? Sure. It doesn't make any more sense for me to be afraid of the entire population of a city than it does for someone to think all gays are sex-crazed perverts. Natural? You bet. Remember, hunkering down behind the barricades is a common reaction to prejudice. I work to overcome that sort of kneejerk reaction, but it's hard work. It's hard work to establish alternatives to polarization, alternatives to demonizing or making scapegoats of any group.

There has been much too much polarization lately, much too much looking for scapegoats and far too little cooperation. Polarization based on prejudice against any group of citizens is not going to help us solve our most pressing social problems. It is not going to improve race relations. It is not going to integrate and improve the quality of our public schools. It is not going to solve our fiscal problems. It pushes us further apart at a time when we desperately need to come together. That is a price we should not be willing to pay.

Chapter Seven: Violence Begets Violence

It's pretty easy to get attention by attacking symbols that have strong emotions attached to them. When I was an undergraduate at the University of Wisconsin-Madison in the mid-1960s, someone took a carefully lettered stencil and a can of spray paint, and covered a construction fence in the heart of the campus with the question "Where is Lee Harvey Oswald now that we really need him?" I was sickened and offended, as were others like me who were struggling to make sense of having friends who were fighting in Vietnam as well as friends who were conscientious objectors. It certainly didn't convince me the war was wrong. I later became convinced, but never condoned the protestors who were promoting the violence they condemned.

Vandalism in a cemetery is certainly going to get peoples' attention, and it did. I doubt it convinced anyone who voted for Amendment 2 to change his or her opinion, and it may have had the opposite effect. That's a predictable outcome given the nature of the symbols being attacked. Picture this: a cross is burned on the lawn of the Metropolitan Community Church, or a swastika painted on the door of the Gay and Lesbian Community Center of Colorado. Would you be upset? Angry? Ready to punish the perpetrators? I sure would. There's no reason to suppose the people upset about the cemetery vandalism are any different.

I have yet to see any evidence that using violence leads to constructive change, or to anything other than more of the same. The prosecutors in the cemetery vandalism case are busy playing politics with the case and fanning the flames of prejudice (If you believe it's a coincidence that the indictments were announced the day the Pope arrived in Denver, I have a bridge in Brooklyn I'd like to sell you). That's not okay, but it is predictable.

Do you want people to be angry or thoughtful? I want them to be thoughtful. I think the leaders of CFV should take responsibility for the results of using the video The Gay Agenda, for the hate it generates, and each of us has to take responsibility for the predictable consequences of our behavior.

Now, I also agree with the columnist Clarence Page that condemnation alone is not enough. He was talking about Louis Farrakhan's anti-Semitism when he wrote that "we also need to listen to and address the frustration to which Farrakhan speaks." Society has the same obligation to its lesbian and gay citizens, the obligation to listen to and address our frustration. Further, when I say that we have the responsibility to express ourselves nonviolently, it is with the clear assumption that we have the right to express ourselves and our frustration.

Violence begets violence, and violent acts, whether verbal ones like calling Colorado "the Hate State," symbolic ones like flag burning, or direct attacks on people and/or property are counterproductive if our goal is for people to behave more humanely and respect

Alice Walker reminds us "Remember always the present you are creating. It should be the future you want." If we want to be treated respectfully by the rest of the world, we had better practice what we preach.

Chapter Eight: Tired

I'm a very tired psychologist. I've spent most of my time since November 3rd helping people deal with the emotional pain caused by the passage of Amendment 2. I've seen clients, friends, colleagues of all sexual orientations in emotional distress. I've had friends chased by gaybashers carrying a broken beer bottle. I've had clients ask why it passed and not had a good answer for them. I've heard stories that several school districts have been asked for lists of single teachers, with the clear implication that the gay and lesbian teachers should be targeted for dismissal, but no media investigative coverage of those stories. I've seen too much pain. Fortunately, I've also experienced a tremendous amount of support, and I've seen people coming together to find ways to combat the prejudice that led to Amendment 2.

I have many reasons to be tired, but what I am most tired of is being lectured by the media. I'm tired of being advised not to participate in "in your face" political action and be more civilized, when supporters of Amendment 2 are busy harassing television stations that report the truth about the legal impact of the amendment. I'm tired of the press minimizing the emotional impact of the amendment. Yes, legally we're where we were a few years ago. Emotionally we are not. I'm tired of being told that lesbians and gays are the recipient of a backlash instead of homophobia, as if that were any less dangerous. I'm tired of being told gays and lesbians aren't entitled to the same protection as members of ethnic minorities because our history is different. No, we weren't brought to this country in chains, and that was a horrible thing. We were, however, left in concentration camps in Germany in 1945 by U.S. troops who released and cared for all the other survivors of those camps. That was also horrible. I'm tired of being lectured by people who are old enough, as I am, to remember that the same language used to justify Amendment 2 was used to justify anti-Semitism and racism in our lifetime. I'm also tired of editors and columnists who write as if the lesbians and gays are a monolithic group who have no internal disagreements about political strategy and should therefore be held accountable for each other's behavior. I'm tired of looking over my shoulder for fear of my physical safety every time I go to a gay or lesbian office or business.

This type of letter is about as close to getting in anyone's face as I get. I'm not sure exactly what a 'militant homosexual' is, so I don't know if I am one. I know that I'm closer than I was on November 2, because I'm now wearing a pink triangle every day. I saw a sign at a rally the other day that said, "Just another tired middle-aged lesbian taking time off from work to fight bigotry." Me too.

Chapter Nine: Looking for Home

It's hardly news that lack of sufficient nurturing is bad for your mental health. We all need a place called home, a place that feels warm and fuzzy and safe. When the usual places called home reject us, when families of origin, home cultures, our own governments do not feel safe, we create alternatives. It is no accident that our code word for another gay man or lesbian is "family." Lesbians and gays have learned to create families of choice, to create safe places, alternative homes. We have learned to do so out of necessity.

When I think about our families of choice, I think about the pride parade last June. I was one of the hundreds lining the last block of the parade route, just before the turn to the capitol steps. As the beginning of the parade approached, the crowd stood almost in unison, rising to greet the marchers, welcoming them home. I saw people with signs saying, "real families value love and acceptance" and another reading "we are all family." Two men were parading with a "Just Married" sign, and two women proclaimed, "We are a family." Adolescents marched with a sign with asking: "Where are your family values when a lesbian or gay teen suicides?" There were drag queens and dykes on bikes: people like them, people so far out they had nothing to lose, stood up to the police at the Stonewall Inn in 1969. They started our civil rights movement while the rest of us crouched in our closets. It felt warm and supportive to be surrounded, the day after the death of a dear friend, by 30,000 marchers who know what it is like to lose someone they love to a disease our government ignored for years because queers and drug addicts are the primary victims.

That parade was the largest gathering of lesbians and gay men in Colorado since I've lived here, probably the largest ever. It felt warm and fuzzy and safe. It is no surprise that we turned to each other for comfort, for warmth and safety, after Amendment 2 passed. The places that were crowded were the ones that felt homey: some were bars, some were restaurants and coffeehouses, some were organizational offices, some were spiritual gathering places: all, in some way, feel like home.

Unfortunately, that initial post-election coming together was short-lived. It was followed by a divisive period characterized by a rush to affix blame for our electoral loss, a finger-pointing period that served our opponents' purposes more effectively than our own. I've begun to see signs we are beginning to move past that self-destructive period. I do not expect it to be easy, but I believe we must find ways to keep communication open even when we disagree, we must find ways to analyze our mistakes without labeling those who made them forever the enemy.

It's almost time for the next pride parade. It will have, I suspect, a very different flavor from its predecessor. Last year we were gearing up for the battle. This year we are licking our wounds and settling in for the long haul. Our parades recognize what we all know: what we share is a differentness that others devalue and a refusal to devalue ourselves. Sometimes that is all we share, and the best we can do is value ourselves and each other and acknowledge our disagreements. Sometimes, and we need more of them, we can make common cause and find ways to agree in part, knowing that we will never come to complete agreement.

That, finally, is what our struggle for civil rights means to me: we are all entitled to a place that is warm and safe, even when we disagree - a place called 'home.'

Chapter 10: What You Can Do to Help

Since Amendment 2 passed, many of my heterosexual friends and colleagues have asked me what they can do to help reduce prejudice and create civil rights protection based on sexual orientation. Here are some suggestions.

1. Read the gay and lesbian publications. Talk about the issues with your friends, family and colleagues. Let other heterosexuals know you have gay, lesbian and bisexual friends, and let them know how much Amendment 2 affects your friends.

2. Don't let anyone get away with stereotyping or tokenism. For example, if you hear someone say they'll vote for Amendment 2 if it comes up again because of the recent desecration at a Catholic church, point out how unfair it is to blame all 300,000 lesbian, gay, and bisexual Coloradans for the acts of a handful of extremists.

3. Wear a pink or black triangle, or a supportive button (e.g. Undo Two, I Wish I Was a Black Bear). Visible symbols are terribly important, both to keep the issue in the public eye and to show support to the bisexuals, gays and lesbians who will see it (and many will notice even if they say nothing).

4. Check on whether your workplace and any organizations to which you belong have nondiscrimination policies with respect to sexual orientation. Make sure those policies are well-publicized. Lobby for passage of new policies where needed.

5. Call or write politicians and reporters who talk and write about sexual orientation issues. Thank those who are supportive and those who provide thorough coverage. Don't underestimate the opposition. They are well-organized, well-financed, and have strong ties to national religious right groups. They call in large numbers when they want to put pressure on the media or on politicians.

6. Remember language is important. Do refer to sexual orientation. Avoid using 'sexual preference' or 'lifestyle.' Both imply sexual orientation is a fad.

7. Challenge the use of economic jealousy to justify bias. There are continuing attempts to portray gays, lesbians, and bisexuals as affluent and therefore not disadvantaged or in need of civil rights protection. First, it is absurd to suggest all of us are affluent. Second, financial resources, when we do have them, do not protect us from discrimination in housing, credit, and employment.

8. Keep letting us know you care. The work, as Mayor Webb reminded us the morning after the election, is life-long. So is the stress. No matter how strongly we believe in making common cause, sometimes we are tempted to huddle behind a barricade in a well-defended ghetto and treat others as the enemy. Your outstretched hands are the antidote.

Chapter 11: The Long Haul

By the time you read this it will have been a month since Judge Bayless declared Amendment 2 unconstitutional. The day of Bayless' ruling the papers were also full of news about Vladimir Zhirinovsky, who was leading in the Russian elections. He doesn't care if he's called a facist or a Nazi, because, he says, there's nothing like fear to make people work better. Here's another of his gems: "Those who have to be arrested will be arrested quietly at night. I may have to shoot 100,000 people, but the other 300 million will live peacefully." I hope this sounds scary to you: It sure sounds like Germany in the 1930s to me.

Unfortunately, many of our fellow citizens don't know much about Nazi Germany. According to a recent survey, thirty-eight percent of adult Americans and 53 percent of our high school students don't know what it was. Twenty-two percent of Americans think the Holocaust might not have happened, might be fiction, compared to five to seven percent of British and French survey respondents.

I don't have a single doubt the Holocaust happened. The only reason I'm here today is that my grandparents left Eastern Europe in the early 1900s. Six million Jews were killed, along with a smaller but still appalling number of gay men and lesbians, Gypsies and political dissenters, and other folks the Nazis labeled undesirable. I have friends whose parents were in the concentration camps. My tailor was in them as well.

For all of recorded history, groups of people have found ways to discriminate against and attack other groups of people. I'm descended from people who have kept their bags packed for thousands of years because they keep getting eviction notices or death sentences, and that's just one small piece of the picture. The last few hundred years have not been kind to the people who came to this country chained to slave ships, nor to the original property owners of the land on which we currently reside, who were summarily evicted in a rather bloody fashion.

You may be wondering why I'm sounding like a wet blanket when we have cause to celebrate—and we do have cause to celebrate. But we also have reason to put Bayless' ruling in the broadest possible historical context. Humanity is good at finding groups to make into scapegoats and lousy at peaceful, cooperative residence on the planet. In addition, we are very skilled at ignoring and denying the inhumanity and suffering we cause each other. Right now, queer folks are one of the primary targets of choice in this corner of the world, but there have been and will be many other targets, and there are always people like Zhirinovsky who are ready to divide and conquer. We need to remember the Holocaust, remember the slave ships, remember the gaybashings because history has a nasty way of repeating itself.

The message, my friends, is that we need to be in this for the long haul, in it till we figure out how to make peace with each other, in it even if it becomes ok to be queer, because it won't end until it ends for everyone.

Chapter 12: Opening the Window of Hope

The Holocaust has been in the spotlight recently, thanks to "Schindler's List." It's been chic to be lesbian or gay. This year, this month, it may be "in" to hear about gays and lesbians, and to remember the horrors of Nazi Germany, but I don't trust fads. Andy Warhol was right about the public's short attention span.

Education, ongoing education, we're often told, is the antidote. Remember the evils of the past so that they will not be repeated. Never forget, or it will happen again.

Remembering, however, is not enough. Remembering is only the beginning. The next steps are listening to and talking with people, creating a world where it's not possible to put anyone into a box labeled "not human," not possible to lynch anyone, not possible to rape anyone, not possible to shoot down a crowd of peaceful protesters, not possible to march anyone into a gas chamber, not possible because we recognize our connections, our common humanity.

Making connections isn't easy. We're much better at competing than cooperation, much better at talking than listening. Moreover, it is particularly difficult to connect with people who are different from us, different in any way that is unfamiliar, unknown and therefore scary. That's why coming out is so important: so everyone will know, live and in person, people whose sexual orientation is different from their own. That's why connecting with people of different races, different religions, different genders, different abilities is so important.

Sometimes understanding each other and making connections is just plain hard work. Occasionally it's much more. On April 9th, at the Temple Buell Theatre, it was much more. That evening Harmony: A Colorado Chorale, our own mixed chorus, hosted an evening of African and African-American music. They called it "A Window of Hope." Ulozi

Inc., a collective of African-American visual artists, had their work on exhibit in the lobby. Performing with Harmony were the Movement Free Dance Company, the percussion ensemble Congueros Del Alma ("Drummers of the Soul"), singer and musical scholar Dr. Arthur Jones, members of the choir from the New Hope Baptist Church, and members of The Eulipion Theatre Company. The Eulipions performed an excerpt from their current production, Langston Hughes' "Tambourines to Glory."

We've all attended events with noble purposes. Some have been merely bearable, some good, a few excellent. "A Window of Hope" was one of the most exciting evenings I've spent in a theater in a long time. It was fun, it was joyful, it was exhilarating. We need more evenings like that, more joyful times to balance the hard ones that are an inevitable part of the struggle to connect.

Here's a painless way to keep the joy happening: call the Eulipions and reserve your tickets for "Tambourines to Glory." Don't go because it's a part of building bridges, though it is. Don't go because it's cool, or the thing to do, though it may be. Don't go to thank all the talented artists who contributed to "A Window of Hope," though they deserve our deep appreciation.

Go, because it's worth a lot more than it will cost you. Go, because we all need more joy in our lives. I'll see you there.

Chapter 13: From There to Here

Pridefest is over and National Coming Out Day is here. Both were unthinkable in 1950 when the Mattachine Society was born. Unthinkable in 1955 when the Daughters of Bilitis was born. Unthinkable when the drag queens fought back in 1969 at the Stonewall Inn. Barely possible when Society and the Healthy Homosexual and Sappho Was A Right-On Woman were published in 1972.

Now I look at the books piled up in my office and see Positively Gay, Lesbian Couples, Intimacy Between Men, Families We Choose, and Gay and Lesbian Families. While there's still far too much hurt and pain caused by prejudice against good people who happen to be lesbian or gay or bi, the world is clearly more welcoming than it was 50 years ago.

Those are books by mental health professionals, but we didn't get from there to here with the mental health professions leading the way. We got from there to here because political activists led the way. In the beginning of a political movement only the very brave or those who are fed up or have nothing to lose lead the way, people like the drag queens at Stonewall, Harry Hay and the Mattachine Society, Del Martin and Phyliss Lyon with the Daughters of Bilitis. More of us join them as we see what they've made possible.

The activism of the last 50 years hasn't happened in a nice smooth progression. Instead, it's been long periods of chipping away at the barriers punctuated by shorter bursts of intense activity. The years immediately after Stonewall were an intense time. So were the Amendment Two years.

It is a great relief to be able to look back at the Amendment Two years with a little less emotion and more perspective than was possible while the battle was still being fought. Prior to that time most of us had developed ways to cope with and limit the amount of prejudice we acknowledged and dealt with on a daily basis. Amendment Two upset the apple cart of avoidance and polite secrecy we relied upon.

Dr. Betty Berzon described that secrecy as a social contract in which we agree not to talk about who we really are. Society then agrees not to withhold respect, admiration, jobs, and affection. In exchange, we don't force others to acknowledge, in Berzon's words, "the awful reality of homosexuality in their midst."

Amendment Two changed all that. It rendered our old strategies useless because none of us could avoid the prejudice. You can't avoid difficult truths when you and your friends are getting hate mail, being chased by thugs with broken beer bottles, having obscenities shouted at you on election day, and receiving death threats.

Fortunately we also came face to face with a considerable number of good people who found the prejudice just as intolerable as we did. We found support from colleagues, friends, relatives, members of the clergy, politicians. And, because we felt less isolated, because we found the prejudice unacceptable and the support heartening, we became more public and more organized. We became less and less willing to collude with those who would make us second-class citizens, more and more willing to say we'd had enough.

I'm not trying to be Pollyanna here. I'm descended from people who've spent the last 5,000 years with a bag packed because they never knew when it was going to be necessary to leave to survive. We can never afford to be complacent, for it is always too easy to make those who are different the common enemy.

I also know there is a downside to making prejudice more public, to violating the social contract that keeps us hidden. Gay-bashing, rejection by parents, loss of employment, and eviction may not be as common as they were 50 years ago, but they still exist and they still hurt. In the short run, the price of exposing bigotry to the light of day is often increased pain.

Nonetheless, I would not for one minute take us back to the dark days of the 1950s. Secrecy is not healthy, and it allows the bigots to flourish. Education and activism are the antidotes. At its best, political activism enlarges our possibilities. Political activists have given us the possibility of being openly gay and keeping our jobs, the possibility of having happy lesbian relationships, the possibility of having a career and being bisexual, the possibility of being mentally healthy, the possibility of being parents.

I was a child in the fifties, but I remember enough of those witch-hunting times to have an enormous respect for the activists who came out and organized in the midst of the hysteria. We owe them a debt that can only be repaid by carrying on and expanding their work, by passing on and enlarging the possibilities for the next generation.

Chapter 14: The Real, 'Normal' Lives of Gays

(Note: This essay was published in The Denver Post Nov. 8, 2000.)
No matter how much things improve, the gay-bashers are always with us. As usual, gay-bashing showed up in a variety of election campaigns around the country this fall.

In the example closest to home, a Colorado for Family Values brochure accused Democratic state Senate candidate Sue Windels of both promoting "the radical homosexual agenda" and voting to allow pedophiles in our schools.

The CFV brochure contained a picture of two women kissing, which I gather was supposed to be offensive.

I'm not going to take CFV to task for the brochure; this newspaper has already done so. My goal is to provide a reality check.

One of the myths behind gay-bashing is that lesbians and gays are abnormal perverts who spend all their time obsessing about and engaging in sexual activity. I'm going to give you the real scoop about the lives of one very small sample of lesbians and gays. The names and some identifying details are fictitious; the concerns are not.

- Sandra's worried because it's a hard time for her adolescent daughter, whose elderly cat is dying.

- Marsha and Joan are wholeheartedly sick of having their house torn up and hope the contractors will be done with the remodeling soon.

- The home study for Martin and Doug's adoption went well, and they're very excited because the adoption agency is now actively looking for a child for them.

- Roy, Lori and Maria's 5-year-old, fell on the playground last week and broke several bones, so they've spent lots of time in medical clinics. I'm happy to report Roy's injuries are healing well.

- Health insurance is on Clarice's mind; She'd like to leave her current job, but it provides excellent health insurance. She feels stuck because her medical problems will make it hard to get coverage elsewhere.

- At my house, we're busy deciding on baby shower gifts for my partner's co-workers.

All of us work full-time, most in the helping professions, education or in non-profits, and one is a small business owner.

Election worries have been a frequent topic of conversation, but CFV will be disappointed to hear no one's talked much about sex lately (we do talk about it sometimes).

What we talk about, like most people, is the fabric of our lives, a tapestry woven out of work, home and people, concerns great and small.

My friends and I are decent people who live ordinary lives, distinguished from the majority only by the nastiness we endure from people with more prejudice than sense and more interest in other people's sexual proclivities than is good for them.

I am weary of the ongoing struggle to counteract the hatemongers' work, but the need never ends. There will always be those who want scapegoats to blame for their problems or to make them feel superior; there will always be those eager to tell everyone else how to act; and there will always be people willing to nurture hate in order to get power. I may have to defend myself from them, but I refuse to let them set standards for me to live by.

If I'm going to be judged, let it be on whether my word is good, if I treat people decently, or if I have a good sense of humor. Look at what I've done to help a child, whether I've made the world a better place in some small way. Ask the only question worth asking about my relationship with the woman I love: whether I've loved her well enough and whether she's done the same for me.

In other words, the content of my character is what matters. Dr. Martin Luther King knew that; CFV, obviously, does not.

Chapter 15: Loving Against the Odds

I am always saddened by Valentine's Day media coverage in the community-at-large, saddened by the omission of so many of us who love in different ways, of so many of us who love against the odds. I remember the woman I knew in college whose Orthodox Jewish parents declared her dead and mourned for her when she married a man who was not Jewish. I think of the interracial couples I've known who've been ostracized in both home cultures. I remember my friend who, for two and a half years, spent his days helping people with AIDS get the services they needed and his nights caring for his partner with the same disease.

Most of us were raised, as I was, to love only within certain socially acceptable boundaries. I was taught commitment was important, but only with Jewish men. For others it meant people of a different race were not approved mates, or those of a different social class. It almost always meant people of the same gender were unacceptable. When we step outside of the constraints we've been taught, it's because love doesn't always fit between the lines.

Many commentators were shocked and offended by the mass wedding conducted in conjunction with the recent March on Washington for Lesbian, Gay and Bisexual Rights. I wonder if they really thought about the meaning of that event. The people who stood together in couples and took wedding vows, women with women and men with men, were demonstrating that they learned the same lessons I did about the importance of commitment. They were demonstrating their belief in the value of family.

Those were people willing to invest time and thought in making their relationships work. And they were people who take those lessons seriously and apply them to the love they found, even though it places them outside the boundaries they were taught to observe.

Here is what I would say to the critics who profess to be shocked by our vows and commitments. You can't have it both ways. You can't claim we're incapable of making commitments, claim our love contributes to the breakdown of the social fabric, and at the same time refuse to honor our commitments. You can't preach respect for one's partner and lasting vows from every pulpit and then profess horror when we do what you've been saying the world needs more of. And you cannot expect to promulgate all those mixed messages without having your hypocrisy named. Moreover, I find it hard to believe there is a deity who would deny people comfort and safety because they do not love in a prescribed fashion. There is entirely too much pain and tragedy in the world already. I'm no theologian, but I cannot believe there is any harm or sin in celebrating love and building a family.

So here's to all of us who take love where we find it, and make families however we can.

A heartfelt Valentine's greeting to us all.

Chapter 16: Change in My Lifetime

I had gotten so used to thinking same-sex marriage was impossible, so used to being outside looking in the window, so used to being the perpetual outsider, that I hadn't realized how much it hurt to be excluded. You would think I would have known. I am fairly sophisticated about these kinds of outsider issues, a psychologist who used to have a psychotherapy practice that focused on meeting the needs of lesbian and gay people. But I just flat out missed it because I had gotten so accustomed to being on the outside, so convinced that I'd never live to see it. You live as if it's never going to happen and is therefore not worth discussing or wishing for. The political climate certainly has not seemed promising, with so-called Defense of Marriage laws, both nationally and in 38 states, that define marriage as heterosexual.

In June of 2000 my partner and I registered with the city and county of Denver as being in a committed relationship. This was notable mostly for the great pains the bureaucracy took to make sure we understood that this act did not entitle us to any legal benefits whatsoever. When Vermont started sanctioning civil unions in July of 2000, it was a significant improvement over the lack of legal recognition provided by our domestic partnership registration. However, I couldn't get very excited because Vermont's civil unions were going to be legally useful only in Vermont; it was unlikely other states were going to rush to create similar laws, and it seemed a pretty glaring example of separate but not equal.

Then a long pause. Life went on, was full, I did not attend to the legal efforts to make same sex marriage a reality. And then it started coming closer. On June 10, 2003, the Ontario, Canada Court of Appeals ruled that equality provisions in the Canadian Charter of Rights and Freedoms invalidated laws that limited marriage to heterosexual couples, and the city of Toronto started issuing same-sex marriage licenses. That, because I grew up in Detroit where Canada was about a half-hour away, brought the possibility much closer.

And then the Massachusetts Supreme Court, on November 18, 2003, ruled that same-sex and opposite-sex couples were entitled to equal marriage rights and gave the state 180 days to change the marriage law it was declaring unconstitutional. Same sex couples rejoiced, and the opposition went nuts. The world was coming to an end and heterosexual marriage would suffer irreparable damage if all us queer folks tied the knot. I was not impressed. Heterosexual marriage is already in serious trouble, no thanks to us.

And I'm tired of being discriminated against. Yes, we can get powers of attorney and make wills and write living wills, and that doesn't begin to give us the legal protections every heterosexual couple has from the day they say "I do." I'm tired of the incredible ignorance that exists about the legal protections that our relationships do not have.

Back to marriage and progress. After the Massachusetts decision, other cities and counties around the country started issuing marriage licenses, most notably San Francisco (of course—where else?). None were legal or likely to provide anything more than symbolic value, but the pictures of hundreds of same-sex couples lining up for licenses certainly put an end to the stereotype that we're all swishy hairdressers, drag queens, or very butch women. Instead, the pictures showed us as we are: a cross-section, from all ages and all walks of life.

By the time the first legal marriage license was issued in Massachusetts on May 17th, it seemed anticlimactic.

Until I was on the way to work the next day and it hit me.

There is now a place in my own country where I can walk in with another woman, ask for a marriage license and be handed one that is legal. Where a justice of the peace (this is about civil marriage, folks, not religious) can actually conduct a marriage ceremony for us. That makes me more a part of the body politic, more fully included, than I have ever been in all my 57 years. Oh my.

I did not expect to see it in my lifetime. I know it faces a whole host of legal challenges and may well not be legal for most of the time I have remaining, But still, I've lived to see it become possible and will not ever again forget how easy it is to become accustomed to being treated as less than human.

It seems like it happened so fast, and yet people have been working to make it happen for a very long time.

Chapter 17: Building a Life Together

Meeting potential mates was simpler in my parents' time, especially if you were heterosexual. My parents were introduced by a rabbi at a Jewish social event while he was home on leave from the Army in 1943. They were married the following year: he was 23 and she was 19, and they stayed married until he died 37 years later.

It took me a little longer to find permanence. I started to realize that I was a lesbian when I was 24 and met my first partner later that year. It was wonderful and confusing, though more for her than for me. Once I figured out that I was drawn to women rather than men, I was thrilled to finally understand what all those love songs were about. I didn't come all the way out of the closet: that was a gradual process—but I never thought there was something wrong with me. My partner had more of a struggle. She had been a nun for eight years and had only left the convent a year before we met. She'd been taught that homosexuality was a sin and that nuns should not engage in "particular friendships."

We had few possessions and no experience with being coupled or being out. Building a life together was new and exciting and we had no previous experience to draw on, only the examples set for us by our parents and friends.

We were together for over twenty years and had a lot of good times and difficult ones, but we never learned to have the kind of open, productive intimate conversation that creates a foundation you can lean on when times are hard. She ultimately left me for another ex-nun whom she'd known in the convent and left me shocked and shattered by an outcome I'd never expected.

I was single for over two years after that. I met my next partner at a lesbian social group and found myself repeatedly asking her to dance and making conversation whenever I could. I was caught by the intelligence shining out of her green eyes. We had a lot in common, many shared interests and values. It lasted for five years and ended for a variety of reasons. One of the lessons I learned is that shared interests and values aren't enough if you don't like to do the same things after work. She was an avid cyclist, competed in at least two triathlons every year and ran the occasional half-marathon. I work out regularly but am not otherwise interested in athletic pursuits. While I liked the people in her cycling group, I tired very quickly of endless discussions about what kind of brakes to use and the best bicycle manufacturers. This difference wasn't the only problem, but it was a deal killer.

Then Penny and I met online in November 2012 when I was 65 and she was 66. I almost didn't respond to her profile: I liked what she'd written, but her picture was of someone who did not look happy. I read it to a friend who'd known me for nearly 30 years, through both my previous relationships. She said, "That's what you've been looking for."

Penny knew she was a lesbian from childhood: I figured it out in my mid-twenties. We both had had other long-term relationships that had good times and were also missing something. We both were delighted to find the partnership we'd longed for, one that gave us the chance to use what we'd learned in the past and create something that would be joyful and life-long.

We were married in July of 2013. At that time same sex marriage wasn't legal in Colorado, and I had a brother and sister-in-law in northern New Jersey, so we married just over the border from there in New York, where it was legal. (Note: A U.S. Supreme Court ruling in June of 2015 made same sex marriage legal nationwide.)

I was living in Denver in a good-sized one-bedroom apartment. Penny lived in a house in Colorado Springs that she'd owned for a long time. Both our respective homes were filled with the furniture and books we'd accumulated over our lifetimes. Following our wedding, in the fall of 2013, I moved in with her in Colorado Springs.

Building a life together is very different when you're older. You have more experience, some good, some not. You have a lifetime's worth of possessions and doing things a certain way in a certain environment. She had three beagles and had always had multiple dogs, usually beagles.

It's whole new world to create a relationship in your late 60s, to finally have someone who listens and talks. However, sometimes it's hard for me to hear what she's telling me, either because I'm too caught up in what i want or because she's not telling me clearly or both.

Part of my problem is selfishness. Part is that she goes back and forth between giving me grief and saying what she needs, and sometimes it's hard to tell the difference. Part is that it's hard to truly comprehend how important dogs are to her, and how well she does without people, since I need people contact, even if much of it is not about intimate friendship but about sharing common interests or doing good together. And i love my cat, but not in the intense way that Penny loves the dogs,

But what an amazing thing it is to have a partner who talks and listens, even though we both are not as good at it as we'd like to be. One of her best features is how well she listens. I wish i was better at it.

Would i be better off single? I'd be more in control, but lonely. I would not have someone to come home to or share my bed with or go to dinner with or make love with or ...that wouldn't be living—I'd have more of a social life, more time to be activist, but no one to share it with.

That is not what i want the rest of my life to look like.

Chapter 18: Devil in the Details

So the fight for same sex marriage appears to be won. What's next for those of us who advocate for full inclusion of lesbian, gay, bisexual and transgender people into society? While there may be a cultural discussion coming about what marriage means, some of us are more focused on the many pockets of prejudice.

Someone once wrote that the most revolutionary question you can ask is: "what do I want?" As a 67-year-old woman who is married to another women, that means being able to live my life with no more fear than anyone my age. We all fear becoming unable to care for ourselves, and many of us fear that we will not have enough money to care for ourselves: I expect to have those real fears for the rest of my life; I can't change those other than to care for myself physically as well as possible and to manage my funds as carefully as possible.

I will be an activist for making it possible for me and my spouse to be treated as well as any heterosexual married couple if we move into an independent living facility, an assisted living facility or a long-term care facility (aka nursing home). I believe that is not likely right now. I was part of a lesbian and gay speakers bureau forty years ago: we (gay men and lesbians) went to college classes, mental health centers and anywhere else we were invited so that the people we spoke to could put a face on the labels "lesbian" and "gay," so that we could have a conversation with people who thought they didn't know anyone who was gay or lesbian. They did know some of us, of course, but not in situations where their friends, siblings, acquaintances, parents or children felt safe in disclosing a major part of their lives.

Now I think that I need to provide that same opportunity to people who work and live in facilities and residences for those of us with gray hair or no hair, who are over 60 and want to live our lives comfortably, without fear that sexual orientation or gender identify will keep us looking over our shoulders. I refuse to go back into a closet I haven't inhabited for decades to make someone else more comfortable.

Chapter 19: Living With MS

Multiple sclerosis (MS) is not as immediately life-threatening as some cancers. It's not as immediately dangerous as a heart attack. It has a different kind of danger. It is unpredictable. It interferes with how information flows in the brain and between the brain and body (fix this). Your spinal cord is often affected and problems with walking are common. You never know when or where it will strike next.

My father was diagnosed with it in his late 40s. He had a form called Primary Progressive MS. That means your symptoms never get better. Sometimes they stabilize for a while, a plateau. Then they worsen. Men with the disease have a harder time with it than women, especially when they're older at diagnosis. Dad's course was hard and fast. He was diagnosed at a time when there was little that medicine could do to keep the disease from progressing or even to mitigate his symptoms: he moved into a nursing home five years after he was diagnosed and died eight years later.

I was diagnosed with MS in 1984, just four years after my father died. I couldn't feel one foot up to the knee, the other up to the ankle. This was a year before Colorado got the ability to use an MRI to make the diagnosis. (Multiple sclerosis means multiple lesions, and those show up on an MRI.) You couldn't have an MRI done in Colorado at that time, so I went through a series of tests that included a spinal tap (a procedure I recommend you avoid, if at all possible). At the time I thought nothing worse could happen to me but soon learned otherwise. After my primary care physician made the diagnosis, I refused to immediately start taking steroids and instead found a neurologist. He was the type of physician everyone should have. The first time he saw me he said, "Your course (of MS) doesn't have to be anything like your father's." I learned to use Progressive Muscle Relaxation, a procedure I later used often with my therapy clients, and within six weeks my symptoms went away.

I had for a long time a form of MS my next neurologist called Benign.

In a few years my body started telling me I needed to urinate even though it wasn't necessary, and I also started leaking, a common symptom called "failure to store." I went on medication for it, and both problems went away. There were a few times when I had "floaters" in my eyes; I took steroids briefly and they went away.

It was 15 years later that I started having problems with tightness in my legs. Leg problems are common in MS, so common that severity is often determined in large part by whether you're still walking. I started a new medication; the symptoms were controlled and I went on my merry way. My legs very gradually became more problematic over the years, and I ended up on three different medications to help relax my leg muscles and manage nerve pain. With the medications I could walk normally. I continued to believe I was going to beat the disease, keep walking and working, and have something other than MS be the cause of my demise. I did in fact keep walking and working until the day I retired after working as a teacher, group home treatment parent, behavior manager, psychologist, technical writer and developmental disabilities specialist for the state of Colorado.

I'm now 30 years post-diagnosis and doing better than almost anyone else who's had MS for that long. However, that was no consolation when last fall my legs became tighter and often painful. My current neurologist and a physical medicine and rehabilitation physician have worked with me to find new medications that help manage the tightness and pain, but my legs, especially the left one, almost never feel normal. This is not good news.

I used to inject myself with Copaxone, one of the new breed of medications that help stop or slow the progression of MS and the one least likely to cause side effects. Unfortunately, I had to stop using it because my skin would no longer tolerate continued daily injections.

Now I've started on another drug that is supposed to have the same effect.

It's hard to take off my blinders after all this time. I still believe something other than MS will kill me first. That's still the plan, but I'm not sure anymore that I can stay as well as I'd like in the meantime. Will I, I wonder, have a wheelchair in my future?

Chapter 20: Keeping My Fate at Bay

I love the medications I take, and I hate them. I love them because without them, multiple sclerosis would long ago have me needing at best a walker and at worst a nursing home due to my legs being too tight to walk unaided without falling over, with constant pain from the tightness. I am grateful that I live in a time when drugs that ease the tightness and end the nerve pain are available and that there are neurologists like mine who know how to prescribe them so that I can stay as functional as possible.

I have eight active prescriptions, plus I take fiber and stool softener for medication-related constipation, plus vitamins and minerals, especially calcium for osteoporosis. Oh, and there's a half pill twice daily for seizure prevention because I've had one seizure in my lifetime. And then there are the eye-drops because I have low-pressure glaucoma, which means I have glaucoma but my eye pressures are in the normal range. An oft-repeated maxim is that growing old isn't for sissies. Neither is growing old with a chronic illness.

I exercise four or five mornings a week, a combination of stretching, strengthening and walking. Those exercises don't change unless I learn something new from an occupational or physical therapist or I do research that turns up something else I want to do.

I'm not as good with diet as I am with exercise. I almost never eat fast food, but I don't get enough fruits and vegetables, and my saturated fat consumption is not as low as it should be due to my fondness for cheese.

What keeps me taking the meds and working out and eating at least semi-sensibly is simple; I know what the alternative looks like. My father had as bad a case of MS as mine is mild. He was diagnosed at 48 and died when he was 61 after spending the last eight years of his life in a nursing home. The odds were against him and are with me. Men who are older when they're diagnosed do worse and women who are younger at diagnosis do better. Nonetheless, I never forget how he looked as he became progressively less able to perform the simplest daily activities, and I'm determined to keep myself in good enough shape that I can avoid that fate or at least keep it at bay for a long, long time.

So most of the time the medications and the worries are a backdrop; nothing to deal with daily except for taking the pills every so often.

Chapter 21: Being Mortal, Being Invisible

Atul Gawande's <u>Being Mortal</u> is a remarkable accomplishment that should probably be required reading for medical professionals. It clearly describes why our current ways of caring for people who are frail, whether due to age or disability, work for society but not for the people being cared for. It also provides alternative visions of how people in need of assistance could be and, in a small number of situations are, provided with care that helps them live as they wish,

The problem with <u>Being Mortal</u> is not what it says but what it leaves out. Gawande acknowledges that people with support systems, specifically those with children, are most likely to stay out of nursing homes Thus he indirectly acknowledges that those who are alone are at most risk for entering nursing homes and having their desires ignored. Given the demographics of the older population, the vast majority of those individuals are women. However, his examples of what happens to individuals as they age are almost all of people with a support system, typically a spouse or children.

There are no examples that describe anyone who is without children or without children who are supportive, and without other nearby supportive relatives. As a 68-year-old woman without children or nearby supportive relatives, I find this omission troubling. There are also no examples or any discussion of what happens to elderly people whose sexual orientations or gender identities are different from the majority. As a married lesbian, I found this omission troubling.

It is the people who have no one to support them or advocate for them who are at most risk for having their wishes for how to live completely ignored and most at risk for entering nursing facilities. Those who do speak up are often punished for questioning their caregivers.

Moreover, I know that many of the nursing home residents whose desires for how to live are not being honored will suffer in silence and never speak up for themselves. Others, like my partner and I, will refuse to go back into the closet and will be faced with the energy-draining need to advocate for recognition of fighting for having their identities and/or their choices being recognized.

Gawande provided examples of alternative approaches to long-term care that are heartening in their descriptions of ways to build care around what is important to those who receive the care. Unfortunately, as he points out, it is extraordinarily difficult to make those models sustainable.

The fundamental question underlying all these issues is how we can create a society that supports all its members, no matter how frail or close to the end of their lives, to live as they choose rather than warehousing them in facilities that serve society and its institutions rather than the people being served.

I am appalled by the number of books and websites that are intended to help the children of aging parents make decisions about living situations for their parents. I have yet to find a resource that addresses what the parents want.

I am left, after reading <u>Being Mortal</u> and considering its implications and omissions, with the questions all of us should ask ourselves:

If I am no longer able to function independently without some form of assistance, who will speak for me? Who will advocate for what I want and try to create it? And, most important, what can I do now to provide me with the future I want?

Chapter 22: Living in Fear—or Not

Fear gnaws at you. It gets in your way. It clouds your thinking. It interferes with having fun, with joy. It's become my constant companion recently without an invitation. Here's what happened.

In the first part of 2014 I ended up in the hospital three times, once for colitis and then twice for a nasty infection called Clostridium difficile (c. diff. for short) Both of those hospitalizations ended with at least a week of rehabilitation so that I could regain my strength—lying in a hospital bed for a week or more is guaranteed to reduce strength and leave you with legs like spaghetti. Physical and occupational therapists came to my home after I left the hospital, so I made good progress toward getting back to normal. Then a few weeks after I came home for the last time, I had the first seizure of my life. I spent a couple of nights in the hospital, added an anticonvulsant pill to my medication regimen and came home. However, I was advised not to drive for 90 days after my seizure, and I was lucky to live in Colorado. In Michigan most people can't drive for six months after a seizure, and in New York it's a full year.

Consequently, I didn't drive from my first time in the hospital for c.diff. until ninety days after the seizure, which came to six months. It took me a while to get used to driving after that. I don't drive a lot because my partner's been driving whenever one of us has a reason to go from Colorado Springs to Denver and whenever we need to go grocery shopping or run other errands together in the Springs. Her 2010 Subaru Forester is a lot bigger and newer than my banged-up 2001 Toyota Camry.

I was just starting to think I should do some of the driving to Denver when I managed to land back in the hospital in mid-April. This time it was for a broken ankle: I got up in the middle of the night to use the bathroom, put my foot down at a bad angle and both sides of the ankle snapped. I have osteoporosis, so my bones are not as strong as the average bear, which contributed to the break. This time I spent three nights in the hospital and two weeks in rehabilitation, learning to walk on one foot with the other knee on a contraption called a knee walker or scooter because I wasn't allowed to put weight on that foot. (The knee walker is a contraption with wheels that had me putting my knee on the seat and then getting around by walking and wheeling.) There are stairs from our garage into the house and stairs going up from the sidewalk into the front door, so going out was a production. I paid a transportation service to carry me, in a wheelchair, in and out of the house when I had an appointment for a checkup on the ankle. Six long weeks later I traded the cast for a walking boot and started navigating on both feet.

The ankle I broke was on my right foot, so no driving yet. It will be at least another three weeks before I can go without the walking boot, and then I'll find out whether I need more therapy and exercise before I can start driving.

In between the c. diff. and the broken ankle, I read <u>Being Mortal,</u> which is all about how badly the medical profession has failed people who are older, who end up being warehoused with their wishes disregarded, especially if they have no family members to care for them. Penny and I are in our late 60s and have no children, so we are at particular risk for that fate. We're agreed that we will stay in our own home as long as possible and hire people to come in when we need help, but the one of us who survives longer is at particular risk for being warehoused. Since we are not independently wealthy but live on state pensions and Social Security, this is not reassuring.

So, fear. Fear about being dependent when I am no longer able to conduct what professionals call independent living skills. The fear is more present now because of my multiple hospitalizations in the last year. We're planning on moving to the Denver area within the next year and will insist that our next house be all on one level both inside and at the exits. That will make it easier to get in and out if one of us has injured a leg, ankle, hip, or any lower body part. However, what happens when we can't drive anymore? Even with help to take care of basics, that's a tremendous loss of independence. Imagine that you are no longer able to go to the store or get, without help, to any place else you're used to going. For instance, I belong to a wonderful monthly book club. No one in it lives anywhere close to where we expect to live.

I could go on, but you get the idea. The fear has always been there, but I realized last week that it's no longer in the background—instead it's ever present. Fortunately, I was finally able to go from having an amorphous cloud of fear hanging over me to realizing that the events of the last year made it a present companion. As I put it together while talking with Penny, she responded by saying, "We can't live in fear." Yes!

Chapter 23: Widow Maker

It was an ordinary Monday afternoon in June in Colorado, warm but not hot and the perfect temperature inside because we'd just had a new furnace and central air conditioning installed. I walked into the bedroom where my wife was folding laundry and she said, "I think I'm having a heart attack." This from a woman who avoids doctors and minimizes her physical problems. I called 911. The dispatcher had me give her four baby aspirin to chew and kept talking with me until the paramedics came. They took her vital signs, did an EKG and said she had to go to the hospital. The ambulance arrived shortly after the paramedics. I told the ambulance driver I had to ride with them: not only did I want to stay with Penny, but I couldn't drive. I was wearing a walking boot on my right leg because I'd cracked a bone a few weeks earlier.

A cardiologist came to see us in the Emergency Department and said Penny needed a cardiac catheterization so that they could identify the problems in her heart. The procedure was scheduled for the next day, and she was admitted to the hospital.

Penny was in a cardiac care unit where she received excellent care, and I was treated with the respect and care that any loved one should receive. This was a great relief after all the years when same-sex couples were invisible at best, couldn't marry, carried health care powers of attorney and hoped they would be honored.

From the hospital, I dealt with the home front. I'd locked the dogs, three beagles, out in the yard before we left the house. Our handyman had been there doing some minor repairs, and I'd asked him to lock up when he left. I called our pet sitter and asked if he could go to the house and feed the dogs. He later came to the hospital and drove me home. I arranged with him to take care of the dogs through the week. From the hospital I called close friends to let them know what was happening.

In other words, I did what I know how to do. I took care of business. I was on automatic pilot. I come from a family where in times of emergency you do what needs to be done, so that's what I did.

But while that was happening, I was also in shock: I was facing the possibility of becoming a widow after being married less than three years. Because it was too overwhelming to sit and contemplate losing her, a part of me was focused on all the logistics that would confront me if she died. Even those practicalities were overwhelming. The reality is that I can't afford to stay in the house alone without Penny's income, and I can't manage the logistics without her; the hauling out of trash every week, the bringing in of groceries up the stairs, especially things like big bags of dog food. And as much as I love those dogs, alone I would not want one dog, let alone three; I'm more a cat person. So I mainly focused on what had to be done to keep things going and get me to and from the hospital.

Tuesday I got a ride to the hospital, and a close friend drove down from Denver to be with us. The cardiac catheterization told us that two of Penny's arteries had blockages and that she needed a double bypass. They scheduled the operation for Wednesday but warned us that it could be delayed a day or two if someone with a more pressing need came in.

I called my mother in Michigan to let her know what was happening and asked her to let my brothers know (one also lives in Michigan, the other lived in New Jersey at that time). I also called friends to give them an update, and I called our rabbi.

Sometime either that evening or the next day before the surgery, someone (I think it was the cardiac surgeon, but I'm not sure my memory is accurate) told me that one of the arteries they were going to bypass was the widow maker. I learned later that this is a common term for the left anterior descending artery. It's called widow maker because a blockage in that artery is often fatal if not treated quickly.

But I did not hear it as just another medical term. I heard, "WIDOW MAKER." And my clear, albeit internal, reaction was equally clear, "I don't want to be a widow!" I do not, for a moment, think that the word was used to deliberately upset me. To the person who used it, it was just another medical term.

I did not need an additional trauma that I might lose her. We already knew that there was a chance, albeit not a large one, that she would not survive the bypass surgery. She coped by telling the people closest to her how much she loved them and by realizing that she was at peace with what she'd accomplished in her life (she's a retired sociology and women's studies professor) and how she'd treated people in her personal and professional lives. I coped by being as supportive for her as possible, by arranging for the dogs and the house to be taken care of and by leaning on good friends.

Finding yourself in the hospital because the most important person in your life is having a heart attack is sobering and surreal. I was trying to be as supportive in every possible way, figuring out how to manage the home front and my own transportation and facing (or not) the possibility of losing her.

It is an unfortunate truism that life isn't fair. What I was sure wasn't fair was that I might lose Penny so soon after I'd found her. She makes me laugh more than anyone I've ever known, and we can talk about anything This is the most intimate and caring relationship I have ever experienced.

The ending was a happy one. Penny had a successful double bypass and will, I hope, live to see many more anniversaries.

Chapter 24: Finding My Way

I am saddened by the state of the country and the world, saddened by the fight over women's reproductive rights, saddened by the multiple wars in the Mideast and the gaps between Israel and the Palestinians and the furor over the negotiations with Iran, saddened by the increasing gap between rich and poor and the influence big money has not only on politics but also on nonprofits and universities, saddened by the large proportion of the general public that places little faith in science and refuses to accept the evidence that climate change is destroying our planet.

I want to live in a country that works. I want to be in a country where my elected representatives work together to find solutions to national and international issues. I want to live in a country where there is an informative public discussion of those issues.

I struggle to try to find some small piece of the chaos where I feel like I can make a difference and where my body will allow me to do so.

I look at where I donate money to find out what matters most to me.

I give to Planned Parenthood because I believe that women need access to affordable reproductive health care, including access to abortion.

I give to Women for Women International because I believe that giving women the tools they need to support themselves is fundamental to their ability to live and thrive. I support Heifer International for the same reason.

I support Emily's List because I believe that one of the surest ways to make politics more responsive to the needs of women and people who need a hand up is to elect more progressive, prochoice women to office.

I support the Colorado Anti-Violence Project because I believe that people of diverse sexual orientations and gender identities should be supported when they are the victims of violence.

I support Disability Law, formerly The Legal Center Serving People with Disabilities and Older People, because I believe people with disabilities and older people deserve high-quality legal and advocacy services.

I support The Gathering Place because it provides homeless women and their children a place where they are valued guests, where they are given sustenance. support and skills to help them feel cared for and gain the ability to care for themselves.

I support the ACLU because it advocates for civil liberties for all, which I believe is fundamental to our system of government.

I support the Southern Poverty Law Center because it teaches tolerance and works against hate and bigotry.

I support Amnesty International because it works for human rights.

I support Common Cause because I support its mission to promote open, honest, accountable government.

I support the Chinook Foundation because it gives support to people who are working toward a just world.

I support Keshet because it advocates for LGBT Jews.

I support Jewish Family Service in Denver because it provides a variety of social services to people in my community.

I am a member of B'nai Havurah because it gives me a sense of community and it has an emphasis on Tikkun Olam.

I volunteer on the Tikkun Olam Committee because I can help provide Tikkun Olam by serving on the Grants Sub-Committee, which is a fit for my professional skills and my desire to help.

I belong to Old Lesbians Organizing for Change because I am an old lesbian who wants to stay connected to other old Lesbians who see value in change.

The lesson is that I care about women, about helping them to help themselves, about giving them access to services that should be available to them and about seeing women who share my political views in elected offices where they can have an impact.

I care about giving people the tools they need to help themselves and also giving them a helping hand when they need one.

I care about people with diverse sexual orientations because I am one of them and never forget that, no matter how much life has improved for us since I realized I was a lesbian, we still have a long ways to go.

I care about advocacy for those who are discriminated against by virtue of disability or age because I am acutely aware that it is advocates, not service providers, who have made real change in the lives of those people and because I am one of them.

I care about fixing our broken economic system so that the rich are not so rich and the poor have food, medical care and decent housing as well as a chance to make a better life. It appalls me that I am privileged and have a lot compared to many others, and yet there are many ways in which I am not privileged.

Afterword

Gail's final years were not what she might have hoped. Penny lived only a few years after her successful heart surgery. After a long illness, Penny died in the summer of 2019 at the age of 73, only six years after she and Gail were married.

Gail subsequently sold their house in Colorado Springs and moved into an apartment in Denver. But her multiple sclerosis was getting worse. She began using a walker, fell numerous times and was in and out of the hospital with a variety of problems.

Eventually she recognized that she could no longer live alone. She moved into an assisted living facility, and after declining further, she transferred to the facility's skilled nursing unit. When the end became inevitable, she was moved into a hospice facility, where she died in July of 2022 at the age of 75.

In accordance with Gail's wishes, her body was disposed of through a process of natural reduction, also known as human composting. At the end of this process, nothing remains except soil, which was distributed to local farms. (Colorado is one of the few states where this is legal.)

Her spirit lives on in the memories of the many people whose lives she touched. I'm sure her personal friends, her co-workers, her many clients and her colleagues in the battle for LGBT rights will remember her as a brilliant, passionate, dedicated and caring person who was often an inspiration to those around her.

Those of us who were her family are left with a lifetime of memories, from the years growing up to the times we enjoyed together as adults – family reunions, vacations at Rocky Mountain National Park, and more.

I cherish all these memories. I am saddened by Gail's passing, and I miss my sister. But I know that hers was a life well-lived, and that the world is a better place for Gail having been in it. I hope this book has captured, to some degree, who she was, and perhaps will help to inspire even more people in the future.